I0167032

SHOOTING TO KILL

SHOOTING TO KILL

A BOOK WHICH MAY SAVE YOUR LIFE

by

ANDREW G. ELLIOT

*A Manual for every Home Guard
and Soldier*

The Naval & Military Press Ltd

Published by

The Naval & Military Press Ltd

Unit 5 Riverside, Brambleside
Bellbrook Industrial Estate
Uckfield, East Sussex
TN22 1QQ England

Tel: +44 (0)1825 749494

www.naval-military-press.com
www.nmarchive.com

"A battle that you think you cannot win, is a battle lost."—FOCH.

"The essence of war is violence, and moderation in war is imbecility."—MACAULAY.

"My right has been rolled up; my left has been driven back; my centre has been smashed. I have ordered an advance from all directions."—FOCH.

"The British have been a free people and are still a comparatively free people; and though we are not, thank Heaven, a military nation, this tradition of freedom gives to our junior leaders in war a priceless gift of initiative. So long as this initiative is not cramped by too many regulations, by too much formalism, we shall, I trust, continue to win our battles—sometimes in spite of our higher commanders."—General Sir A. WAVELL, from *The Times*.

CONTENTS

INTRODUCTION

THIS small book presupposes, on the part of the reader, an elementary knowledge of rifles and other technical matters, such as is possessed by every Home Guardsman and Soldier.

In it I hope to be able to convey the experience I have gained—as a result of having fired a million and a half rounds—in the use of the service rifle and shooting in war conditions, as distinct from the rifle range.

There are two personal matters which I wish to mention. Firstly, I dislike writing a book on warfare, but, under the present circumstances, when Britain is threatened, I feel it my duty to do so. Secondly, I wish to express my sincere thanks to Mr. Robert Churchill for his generosity in permitting me to use certain of his ideas, which he has so admirably expressed in *How To Shoot*, his classic work on shotgun shooting, published by Geoffrey Bles Ltd. Indeed, but for the benefit derived from his volume many years ago, I could never have written this manual.

SHOOTING TO KILL

CHAPTER ONE

YOUR RIFLE AND YOU

*Loading Methods which May Save Your Life—
Wind Allowance*

I AM always amazed at the way in which men
handle their rifles. At almost any Home Guard
parade one can see volunteers unintentionally
pointing weapons at each other, and again, in the
trail position, the rifle is often directed to the man
in front. A rifle should never point at anything
unless the intention is to fire. Of course training,
with aiming discs or blanks, is another matter; but
even so the soldier should be certain that the rifle
is empty, and that his companions have had an
opportunity of examining it. He should, on such
occasions, never carry live ammunition. Further, he
should be consciously aware that, in pointing his
weapon at one of his own men, he is doing something which normally he ought never to do.

This may sound elementary, but having fired
approximately one and a half million rounds, and
having seen others hit and been hit accidentally
myself, I can certainly confirm that rifles do go off.
The excuse is always the same—''I didn't think it

was loaded.'' Accidents are, unfortunately, so easy: someone leaves a bullet in the chamber, the trigger catches on a button or a twig, or through a fall the spring is released. Therefore it is imperative to keep the rifle either pointing to the sky or the ground. When the ''balloon goes up,'' and you are nervous and excited, the one thing you will not do is to shoot one of your own men, if proper habits have been formed. Special care is also necessary when a rifle is being loaded, for it is particularly prone to go off at this time.

Accidents often occur when an enemy is seen, possibly at several hundred yards, and the soldier fires. The cartridge misfires, and the rifleman cannot understand the reason. He explains to a companion that he pulled the trigger and nothing happened. The companion, supposedly more expert, takes the weapon, and the safety catch is found to be on. He hurriedly releases it, and instinctively pulls the trigger. If the rifle is pointing at someone, there is, of course, an accident. If not, the explosion gives your position away. Such warnings may sound stupid, and the reader probably feels he would never do such a thing; but I know from experience that many good shots have behaved similarly in the heat of the moment. One simply cannot be too cautious.

Another point rarely stressed is that the finger should never be on the trigger until the rifle is aimed. Many men mount, that is to say bring the rifle to the shoulder, with the finger inside the trigger guard. This is incorrect and dangerous. The finger should lie alongside the trigger guard until the second of taking aim. Then, and only then, should it be put well round the trigger. War has been described as the greatest of all arts, and rifle shooting is not the simple business which range practice indicates, and many soldiers imagine it to be. Accidents rarely happen in training, but more often occur in action. Then the soldier is excited. With splinters and bullets flying around, his mind may even largely be a blank. It is here that sound training and careful habits bear fruit. Instinctively he will conduct himself correctly.

In case it is felt that I am exaggerating in urging the need for thought, care and training, I will mention that in the Great War, the Germans killed and took prisoner, exactly twice as many of French and British as the Allies did of them. De Gaulle, that master soldier, maintains that it takes six years to make a soldier.* We, in the Home Guard, have to attempt to become effective in a total of as many months.

If invasion occurs, I can foresee many accidents among our members. When the church bells toll, men will load up and move to their positions. If they are wise, and if any of the enemy are expected in the vicinity, they will keep under cover as much as possible. Men creeping along hedges or in the shadows look suspicious. There is a danger, therefore, that some of the raw recruits may think they are Nazis and shoot.

* *The Army of the Future*, by General de Gaulle (Hutchinson).

Care not to shoot until they are sure of identification should be impressed on all Home Guardsmen. In cold blood, cases of mistaken identity would not occur, but when the enemy are among you, it is a different matter altogether. To illustrate this, one has only to point to the number of our own men who were accidentally fired on in the early months of the war, when invasion seemed imminent. Admittedly, the victims were those who failed to respond to challenges, but even so, if the challenger had kept his head, he could have undoubtedly found a way of halting the individual by means other than shooting.

If Nazis are in the neighbourhood, all rifles should, of course, be loaded and *with a round in the chamber*. Everyone should remember to keep the safety catch off. This seems a trifling point, but experienced soldiers will tell you that frequently a novice, being cautious, will keep his rifle at safe. Then, when surprised, he takes aim, pulls the trigger, and there is no discharge. By the time he realizes what has happened, he will, if he is lucky, be in hospital, for a Nazi will not make this beginner's mistake.

On a few occasions, the safety catch is advisable. For instance, in crossing a fence or wall in company with others, and provided immediate action is not required the moment one gets on to the other side. But when one is under fire, the lesser risk has to be taken, and the rifle kept at full cock, on account of the delay in moving the catch. If the catch is put at safe to cross an obstacle, it must at once be put forward to the ready position, and all N.C.O.s in charge should make certain that this has been done. In time, and it is surprising how long it takes, the putting off and on of the catch becomes a habit. In action, one must form this habit of cocking the rifle, otherwise one will be caught napping. I have elaborated this because I know how many lives are lost through neglect.

A matter which I have not heard mentioned, but which is also vital, is the loading technique. This may be the means of saving a soldier's life, or conversely, causing a Nazi's death. The soldier is usually told to load his magazine with five rounds or whatever it holds, and as he fires, to count the rounds so that he will know when to reload. This instruction is insufficient.

Often one or two rounds will be all that are used at a time. While waiting for the next shot, the soldier should fill up his magazine again. If the rifle takes five cartridges, this means that by replacing the two fired, one has five chances of life instead of three.

Quick loading is impossible if the cartridges are carried in the bandolier, so a few clips should therefore be kept in a pocket from which they can be readily extracted.

The moment a shot has been fired the cartridge should be ejected. Many inexperienced soldiers forget their bolt action, and find, on the next occasion, that the rifle fails to discharge. Remember to reload.

This question is one to which great attention

should be paid. Like everything else, it needs practice. Try, therefore, fitting in a clip of cartridges in all positions—standing, lying, running, walking, on your side—and practise it silently for night operations. Do not be content with occasional attempts, but do it hundreds of times until the operation becomes simple and mechanical. For this purpose, dummies are required, but if none are available, use live ammunition. But if the latter, keep quiet about it, and don't pull the trigger; but if the rifle goes off, so long as it is pointed to the sky or the earth, there is little likelihood of accident. Speed in reloading will save many lives.

Much has been said on the subject of keeping the rifle clean, but in action there is one important point to remember. Never allow any mud or dirt to get inside the magazine or barrel, otherwise jamming is likely, which may prove fatal.

In bayonet charges, a round should always be kept in the chamber. There is no danger of this being accidentally discharged since the fingers are not near the trigger at such times, unless the need arises.

This trick has saved many a life, for often during a bayonet fight, an enemy can be seen taking aim at you or at one of your comrades. At close range this is known as firing from the hip. In such cases, as the butt is not against the shoulder, the rifle must be tightly held.

Theoretically, it might be thought impossible in the heat of a hand-to-hand struggle to fire effectively without risk of killing your own men. In practice, however, this is not the case, and there is also time to shoot to prevent being shot, by using the sight-less method which we will later describe. The reach of a bayonet is short, and a bullet may be just the means of saving you. You should fix bayonets when you are likely to meet the enemy hand-to-hand, but don't do 'it before this, as the extra weight makes it more difficult to hold the rifle and so to shoot straight.

The inexperienced will have heard much about allowance for wind, and the effect of rain on the bullet's course. These factors can be ignored. In war, most shooting is at 300 yards or less, and at that range, wind or rain have no perceptible effect. In theory, with a strong wind, at a couple of thousand yards, aim should be taken a few feet to the windward, but in practice, except at very long ranges, it is better to ignore this academic principle.

A common subterfuge of war is for the man who is fired at to pretend he is hit. This trick, whereby the enemy feigns death until the opponent exposes himself, deceives only the tyro. The experienced know when they make a kill. The bullet entering the flesh has a distinct sound which can be recognized, except at very long range. It is rather like the sound of a cigarette packet dropping on to a carpet.

An important factor which the infantryman should remember is, that if he is tired, it is more difficult to shoot straight. Therefore he should never walk if he can ride, he should never, in action, sit down if he can lie and rest. The fresher he is,

B

the more accurate will be his shooting, so when
actions are pending, as much sleep and relaxation
should be obtained as possible.

The Home Guardsman and his rifle, through
abundant familiarity, should become one. Meta-
phorically speaking, the gun should be welded to
you as if it were as much a part of you as your arm
or leg. It is at once your dagger and your shield—
your death-dealer and life-saver. In the following
pages, I shall try to teach you how to shoot without
being shot.

In the invasion of Britain, there will be no quarter
given and we shall surely ask none. It will be you
or the other fellow, for the taking of prisoners will
probably be out of the question for both sides,
except for the purpose of securing information.

LESSONS IN BRIEF

Don't point rifle at anyone.

When loading, point to sky or earth.

Keep a round in the chamber.

Replenish the magazine always.

When you kill a Nazi, don't expose yourself until
the coast is clear.

Practise reloading hundreds of times.

Leave the safety-catch off.

Identify the enemy before shooting.

Forget about wind allowance except for very long
shots.

Form the habit of looking at the bolt from time
to time, as if it is not "home" the trigger
cannot be released.

CHAPTER TWO

INSTINCTIVE AIMING TECHNIQUE

Importance of Timing—Using Rifle as a Machine-gun

WE have mentioned the need for training in loading, but of greater importance is practice in mounting the rifle to the shoulder. Obviously without this, taking aim will be awkwardly accomplished. Yet few musketry instructors emphasize this point sufficiently. The pupil is apt to feel that he is wasting his time with so simple an operation, yet, as we shall see, in the whole technique of shooting, nothing is more vital. The muscles must be properly attuned, and the nerves automatically co-operate with the eye and mind if speed and accurate shooting is to be accomplished.

To illustrate the difference between trained and untrained muscles and nerves, carry out the following small experiment. If you are right-handed, you will generally comb the hair with the comb in the right hand and the brush in the left. Try reversing the process and see what happens. You will find every movement is awkward. If, however, you continued to practise for weeks, your muscles and nerves would form habits, and would soon work instinctively without conscious effort.

It is the task of those who are new to the rifle to

form the habit of mounting it and taking aim. The oftener one practises, the more expert one becomes, but there are certain basic principles which must be followed before perfection can be achieved. There are various positions from which firing takes place in war. Lying, or the prone position is the most common, but leaning over parapets or weapon pits, kneeling and standing are also frequent. In point-blank shooting, and numerous other situations, the standing position is often the quickest and best.

In all these, certain movements occur and it is in these muscular adjustments that training is required. Take the standing position. Everyone knows roughly how to hold a rifle, so all that need be said is that it should be held tightly with the right hand, and the chin should be pressed close to the side of the stock with the butt fitting well into the shoulder. A good grip should be taken with the extended left hand, as all these holds help to keep the rifle steady and prevent the kick from upsetting the aim. Timing is required and, as the trigger is released, the grips should be almost vice-like.

This aiming practice should be done in the house or garden with any imaginary target or targets, preferably with dummies, but the trigger does not always require to be used, for its releasing is the most simple part of the operation. It is primarily muscle, nerve training and forming the correct aiming habit which has to be established.

For the standing position adopt an easy, comfortable stance, the left foot a little forward and at right angles to the right one. The next problem to be solved is the best way to bring the rifle up, and not down, to the target. It should be raised parallel to the ground. At this stage, little conscious attention need be paid to lifting the rifle on to the target.

I am now going to make use of information derived from Robert Churchill's book, *How To Shoot*.* I regard this as the greatest work on shotgun shooting ever written, and all interested in this sport should read it.

The author points out that if someone asks you the way, when you indicate the route with the finger, you do not trouble to look along the arm to make certain that it is pointing in the correct direction. Automatically and instinctively, the finger points at the place you wish to indicate.

Likewise, after sufficient practice, perhaps for half an hour a day for several months, the rifle will be found to point directly at the centre of the target, provided you are looking at the place you wish to hit. After taking this instinctive aim, by all means check up and make sure, that the sights are in line with the target. The reason you are not recommended to rely on the sights, as you may have done at the rifle range, is that in action one rarely has time to take elaborate aims and must depend largely on instincts which are less likely to let one down in an emergency.

The next technique to be explained is—and this

* *How To Shoot*, by Robert Churchill (Geoffrey Bles Ltd.), by kind permission of the author.

is another of Mr. Robert Churchill's points—that when aim is taken, the body, left hand and eye should all be directed towards one thing and only one thing, the target.

I have no objection to using the sights, but for ordinary rifle shooting they are unnecessary, *provided the rifleman has become proficient in aiming and has had sufficient practice.* Of course most soldiers will lack the confidence to shoot without sights, but that does not mean that they should not train themselves to take aim first, and confirm that aim to be correct afterwards. This is the quickest method. Indeed, get your rifle on to your man, and the eye will automatically grasp the sights, if there is time, and if the range makes it necessary. A parallel can be drawn here. If a man can cycle without his hands on the handlebars, he will obviously have greater control of the cycle when he has hold of them.

It cannot be over-emphasized that the body, the eye, the left hand, in fact the whole personality and being should be directed at the enemy, and incidentally at the part of the enemy you wish to hit. At ordinary ranges of a few hundred yards, the bullet goes exactly where the eye is looking, within reason, provided body, arms, eyes, etc., are all co-ordinated.

This is not theory. I, myself, can obtain as good a card by ignoring the sights as when using them, and in war it is as well to remember that the split second often means the difference between killing and being killed. When opportunity permits, the sights can be employed to confirm the initial instinctive aim. If the soldier has practised aiming sufficiently, he will find that no alteration is required.

With regard to the sights themselves, the aperture back-sight allows the eye automatically to do the focussing. The tip of the foresight comes into line with the dead centre of the target, and unconsciously the aim is correct. These aperture sights are almost foolproof.

With **U** or **V** back-sights, the same principle applies. Don't worry about focussing the back-sight. Get the tip of the fore-sight on to the centre of the target and the eye, of its own accord, does the rest. Actually with these open sights, it is the top or tip of the fore-sight which is aligned on the target in a line with the top or shoulder of the **U** or **V** back-sight. It should, of course, be understood that every rifle has its own peculiarities. That is why everyone must obtain practice with live ammunition to observe the results. If the rifle has a peculiarity, it can either be allowed for, or if anything is seriously out of order, for instance the sights sometimes get broken or twisted, the armourer will rectify the fault. If in any doubt at all, rifles should be tested by an expert at a range of a hundred yards. The majority of shots close the left eye, but many good riflemen keep both eyes open. In practice, one eye is usually master, so that with most people it does not affect shooting if both are open, and, incidentally in action, the disengaged eye sometimes sees approaching danger.

The reason abundant practice in aiming is needed is that, in this war, as distinct from the last, speed wins. Trench warfare, lines and so on are abandoned and mass assaults, paratroops everywhere, and infiltration at terrifying pace is the order of the day. There is no time to stand around.

The same practice should be carried out in the kneeling and prone positions, leaning over a parapet, firing round a wall, shooting through a loophole, etc. Practice, indeed, should be continued until the whole business becomes as subconscious as putting on your hat.

The kneeling position is taken up with the right knee, leg and toes on the ground, the left foot on the ground with the leg at right angles to the ground. This enables the left elbow to rest on the left knee, thus steadying the left arm which holds the rifle. This is a splendid stance, for it allows freedom of movement, while presenting a smaller target to the enemy. Naturally one cannot continually hold the rifle to the shoulder, so the practice here consists of bringing it from the ready position up to the shoulder, and taking aim at various imaginary targets. Different angles should be practised, as would happen in action. For instance, if a target presented itself on your extreme left or right, this would necessitate a pivoting of the right knee, and a movement of the left foot, so that, as in the standing position, everything would be directed at the target. The left foot is pointed at it, the right leg is in line with the target, the left hand, eye, and as we have said, the whole person is directed at the object to be hit. The sitting position is an excellent alternative. Here the rifleman sits, mainly on his right buttock, with the right leg tucked under the left knee. Otherwise the position is the same as the kneeling one just described.

In the lying or prone position, the freedom of movement is restricted. In this position, most textbooks advise the soldier that his position will be easier if he lies at a slight angle, which is true. But in war, abandon such armchair theories, unless of course the lie of the land allows it.

The whole idea of the prone position is to present the enemy with a small target. If you are exposed to him, by lying straight towards him you furnish a very small target of only head and shoulders. This, however, is somewhat uncomfortable, so that if you are protected by cover the regular and easier position can be adopted.

The urgent need for practice is in order to strengthen the muscles and gain the habit of speedily mounting the rifle to the shoulder and aiming. This position is a good one if it is known that the enemy is in front, but it is an awkward one if there is any chance of an enemy being at either side, for the soldier presents a larger target. Moreover, in the prone stance, vision is restricted, as is the ability to swing round for a side shot should the need arise. Nevertheless, on account of concealment, it is advantageous in many types of fighting. The great thing to remember is that the holding position should be easy and comfortable, and all movements completely co-ordinated.

If dummies are available, they can be used a few hundred times, but once proficiency is attained with the trigger, there is no need to continue this every time an aim is taken, because of unnecessary wear in opening and closing the bolt.

As to trigger pressing, you will hear much on the range about a first pull and a final pull which discharges the round. In action, this requires little attention, for the whole process becomes instinctive. Usually there is no time to worry about the first pull, and one can only take aim and fire instantaneously.

The reason for the first pull is that if a man is tired or exhausted, and his hand is shaking, the first pull acts as a steadier for the nerves; also for long shots, for which time can be taken, it has some value.

In practising trigger releasing, always be sure you pull directly. You can test this by observing if the rifle momentarily moves to the right as the trigger is released. Naturally, this is fatal to accurate shooting. Put the finger well inside the guard and rather squeeze the trigger than pull it, which prevents throwing the rifle out of alignment.

How often should the beginner practise aiming? He should do so daily for up to an hour in all positions, provided he can spare the time, with an odd day's rest each week for several months. Keep on raising the rifle until the arms are so tired that it is impossible to continue. Then carry on for a little longer. In this way, strength is increased, the muscles, nerves and eyes become accustomed to their task, and after you have practised aiming tens of thousands of times, you will become one of the finest shots in the Army.

If I seem to have placed undue emphasis on this point, it is only because I know that continued practice and experience are the only ways to perfection. When you have mastered the technique, have an odd hour's practice once a week to retain efficiency. It goes without saying that firing practice at rifle ranges is essential, so that the learner can check up and see how he is progressing.   .

I make no apology for having written forcefully, for as the reader is aware, his very life depends upon the speed and accuracy with which he can shoot.

A good test of efficiency would occur when a position is charged. Firing from a defensive post, the experienced rifleman will kill a Nazi for every bullet used. The inexperienced soldier will be bewildered, because, as he would say—if he lived to tell the tale —he had no time to aim. Any shots which he fired would be wild, and would have only slight chance of killing. The experienced and practised shot, on the other hand, should have no difficulty in bagging five Nazis in a charge as short as fifty yards. Pick out your enemy and shoot him.

LESSONS IN BRIEF

Practise aiming tens of thousands of times.

Train in all varieties of position.

Bring the rifle up to the target, not down.

Form the habit of using sights only to rectify aim, if time permits.

The eye, left hand and body should point at the enemy.

Put the finger well round the trigger when firing.

An almost vice-like grip at moment of shooting.

Adopt a comfortable position.

CHAPTER THREE

SNAP SHOOTING—DISAPPEARING TARGETS AND PERSONAL EVASIVE ACTION

Killing without Being Killed—The Snipe Technique

If invasion is attempted, no doubt the main attack will be across the narrow part of the channel, for to attempt to land armies by a longer sea route, with the disparity between the two navies, would be madness. The crossing over the Channel can be strongly protected by U-boats, coastal batteries and aircraft. These main thrusts would be dealt with by the Navy, R.A.F. and Army.

It will be the lines behind the lines where the Home Guard will play its part. The Home Guard is defence in depth in answer to the attack in depth. Doubtless, as has happened elsewhere, certain units will break through our lines and run rampant across the country. These tanks or armoured fighting vehicles will be accounted for by the Home Guard. Parachute troops and crash-landing troop carriers will bring thousands of men to cut communications, spread havoc and panic in all surrounding areas, and possibly throughout the country. If the Germans launched, as is quite possible, 50,000 cheap planes, with only ten men in each, we should have half a million of the enemy in our midst. Hitler would not mind if he never saw

one of these aircraft again. The R.A.F. would knock
out a percentage of these machines, but an even
larger number would get through somehow.

The task of the Home Guard would be tremen-
dous, for they would be fighting desperate men,
most of whom would be fanatical Nazis. In addi-
tion, we would be pitted against the most highly
trained and best equipped soldiers in the world.
Despite the fact that they might be outnumbered,
these men would take a heavy toll, but the result
of the battle would largely depend upon the pre-
paredness and effectiveness of the Home Guard. A
service rifle will kill anything from a Nazi to an
elephant, and provided the Home Guard get blood
on every bullet, or even on every second bullet,
things will be very unpleasant for the Nazis.

Let us try to imagine what will happen in any
given area. Men will land in parties, possibly in the
twilight or the dawn. Their first job will be to link
up with each other. Then they will attempt to carry
out whatever task has been allotted to them, which
may be to take a waterworks, a factory, a railway
station, a road block, a village, a bridge or any
other military objective.

A recent speaker, who was an officer in the last
war and also in the present one, expressed the
opinion that if there was a battle for a certain
village in the North, it might only last a few days.
Balderdash of this kind creates feelings of false
security. The defenders think they will have time
to organize themselves and call for reinforcements.
I am perfectly convinced that the battle for the

average village will be over in a matter of minutes, or at the longest, hours. Transport planes can bring over tanks and vehicles of up to fifteen tons, as well as light artillery. The method employed is to ship the machines in skeleton sections, which are fitted up, and filled with concrete to give the necessary protection and weight. Therefore the Home Guard must be off the mark with lightning speed and prevent these troops assembling, so that organized attacks will never take place, or if they do, time will have been gained for the regular Army units to reach the spot.

Everyone agrees that air-borne troops are most vulnerable at the moment of landing. It takes them half a minute to unharness their parachutes or disembark, and collect their weapons. In the case of the parachute troops, these materials, except for very light weapons, are dropped separately in containers. In these early minutes the Home Guard can, and will, upset the German plans. No class of fighting calls for greater training than hand-to-hand or point-blank, and yet none can be so decisive, especially if one side knows the country. The parachute container can be kept under fire to damage it, and prevent the Nazis using its contents. It will probably be dropped by a parachute of different colour.

In certain instances, it is possible that part of the enemy force will manage to assemble and move off to their objective. Pitched battles will usually be out of the question, but guerrilla, street fighting and harassing tactics will be effective. In other words, point-blank shooting and snap shooting will be the technique. Let us therefore study these two methods.

Point-blank shooting is less easy than it sounds. There are some matters which must instinctively be remembered. At close quarters, bayonets will be fixed for personal defence, but a bayonet is useless at fifteen yards if a Nazi has a bead on you with an automatic pistol. Therefore, as we have said, keep a round in the chamber. Another point to be remembered about this type of warfare is that the soldier is liable to kill his comrades. In the excitement, men are apt to lose their heads, especially if they are unseasoned troops. Bullets go right through a body, and if there is a British soldier behind a Nazi, one shot will kill both. Therefore don't fire till you have a clear aim.

By getting in amongst the enemy, trained and practised men can often play havoc, for he, too, will be scared of shooting his comrades. If the men have practised sufficiently the instinctive aiming methods described in the last chapter, they will not fire wild shots. At this close range, every bullet should kill. Needless to say, there is no time for aiming, and it is advisable that a sharp look-out should be kept. In these instances, Home Guardsmen will be up against automatic pistols and possibly tommy-guns. But there is no cause for alarm. Neither of these are so accurate as rifles. Of course, on account of the number of rounds which can be fired without reloading, these weapons have some advantage, but in point-blank fighting this is liquidated for several reasons.

The Home Guardsman has a bayonet, for which the Nazis have a great aversion, and if he is trained, his five rounds, replenished before they are all used, can prove deadly. We all know the expression "quick on the draw," which is applied to revolvers. but few realize that a rifle can be mounted to the shoulder, aimed and fired in a split second. Experienced riflemen can fire upwards of thirty rounds a minute, and this includes reloading after every five shots. This should be borne in mind by any Guardsman who imagines that he is inadequately equipped, for it is rare that thirty targets will present themselves in one minute. I mention these matters because there is a tendency to despise the rifle. In trained hands it is a good tool. In close range fighting it should be carried between shots, with both hands, half-way up to the shoulder, ready for *instantaneous* discharge at any target offered.

Care must be taken never to bunch together, for men in close formation are the tommy-gunner's dream. Spacing of at least twelve yards, individuality and training are excellent answers to automatic weapons.

Encounters with the enemy may occur in the open, in poor visibility, in woods, in streets and even between houses, some of which may be occupied by Nazis.

Naturally many targets will be of a disappearing nature, and that is why speed is vital. With this snap shooting, as a rule, no aim up to distances of a hundred yards is required. It is rather a case of

c

swinging the rifle into position, and firing, in one speedy movement.

In point-blank warfare, situations frequently arise in which there is one chance of escape—personal evasive action. When being aimed at or under fire, either by a rifle, revolver or even machine-gun, the chance of being hit is reduced by keeping on the move. It is further reduced if the movements are made according to what I shall call the snipe's technique.

The principle for such evasive action is dictated by the snipe in flight. If you have ever seen this bird, which escapes all but the most expert shots, you will understand what I mean. When it leaves the ground, after a few seconds, it immediately flies in a zigzag fashion, so that no sooner is aim taken, than the bird has changed course. Therein lies the secret. If you see a rifle or automatic trained on you, move in zigzag bounds. Run a few steps, then stop, turn or bend down. Jump and run again, but follow the fundamental rule of never allowing your enemy time to focus you. It is useless running straight away or towards your opponent, for that provides an easy target. All this sounds mad, but it is by running about like a raving lunatic that your enemy will be dumbfounded. Unless he is a lightning shot, you are safe, except for an unlucky hit. Such antics are less successful against a machine-gun, but they will increase your chance and make the enemy use his ammunition, which on account of his difficulty of replenishing, he may be disinclined to squander. While the machine-gun or tommy-gun can fire numerous round per minute, these can rarely be fired with much degree of accuracy, and at some point you may be able to obtain a snap shot at your enemy. Practise creates the necessary self-confidence. Here I refer to close in-fighting where there is no cover obtainable.

For this reason, it is essential that section commanders train their men in point-blank shooting. It can be done in a confined area, a white band round the cap representing the enemy. Then, with unloaded rifles, men can aim at each other, and immediately afterwards check whom their shot would have killed, and where it would have gone.

Too much attention is usually paid to ordinary target training at the range. Such training should discontinue the moment a volunteer is able to handle his rifle with safety, for it is well known that many experts at the range are useless in the field.

Certain facts must be impressed on the beginner. For instance, few men realize the speed at which a bullet travels. If a rifle is fired from the shoulder, parallel to the ground, the missile, miles away it must be remembered, will fall to the ground AT THE SAME TIME AS A BULLET OF THE SAME SIZE DROPPED BY HAND FROM A HEIGHT OF FIVE FEET. In other words, a bullet travels at terrific speed, at, I think, over a thousand miles per hour. I mention this to illustrate the fact that in point-blank shooting, after one has been fired at, evasive action is too late. Also, the moment one can get a bead on the enemy, and release the trigger, nothing he can do can save him.

Shooting practice should be carried out under all sorts of trying conditions. For instance, men should be made to run a mile with full equipment to within two hundred yards of a target, drop down and fire five or ten rounds, and the results should be judged, not only for accuracy, but for speed. One bull and the rest inners and outers would be far better shooting than twice or thrice the number of bulls and inners if twice the time was occupied.

Again, good practice is provided if men are made to shoot after a five-mile march with full kit following a Saturday morning's work at the office or factory.

Training should be given in short-range snap shooting. At a hundred yards, a soldier should be able to fire a minimum of twenty rounds in a minute, and get them all on to the target, with a fair percentage of bulls. It is hard work, but it is worth it.

But to attain speed, practice in loading, bolt action, aiming and firing is necessary, until the operation becomes a second nature.

In this shooting, it is better to train men to use the battle sight in preference to the adjustable one, as the former is what will mostly be required in the field. In some rifles, this is set for 400 yards. This means that the bullet is accurate at 400 yards. At shorter ranges, the bullet, owing to trajectory—that is, curve of flight—will hit the target at a slightly higher point. The highest point of the bullet's flight will be at about 200 yards, and here the rise will be only about a foot, depending on the individual rifle. At 100 yards, the rise will be trifling, while at 300, the bullet being on the downward curve, it will only be a matter of a few inches, perhaps three or six.

It is obviously wiser always to shoot low at *short range*.

Therefore, if a man is running towards you, shoot at his middle. There are several good reasons for aiming at a definite part of your opponent's anatomy, for, as we have said, by aiming a few inches low, you allow for the trajectory. Again, the most vital part of the body, apart from the head, which is a small target, is the spinal column. Also, it must be remembered that by aiming at your opponent's head, if you miss by six inches, which is easy in action, you do not kill, for in shooting, a miss is as good as a mile. On the other hand, if you aim just at the middle of his stomach, if you are a few inches out, you will still get your man.

When your opponent is lying on the ground, for short-range shoots, the part one inch above where his body meets the ground is the spot at which to aim. There are other reasons for this than the fact of rise owing to trajectory. For instance, if your aim is low, especially on hard ground, you may still score a hit, for the bullet should ricochet upwards and find its mark. Again, by focussing the aim at this part of the body, provided you aim about six inches away from the armpit, there is a good chance of going through the heart, which, of course, is a vital spot. If the enemy is lying head on, aim for his chin.

These are the rules. Shoot for the spine or the

region of the heart whenever possible. To do otherwise, for instance a hit on the leg, shoulder or arm, means wounding, and since bullet wounds are usually painless at the time, there is always the possibility of your being shot by the same man. The head, of course, kills quickly, but, as we have shown, it is not an easy target, unless at short ranges.

In some instances, of course, heads peering up one second to get in a shot, and down the next, are the only targets offered. These call for fast shooting, such as has been described. Remember, the point at which to aim is just an inch above where the lower part of the exposed head shows itself. (Beware of empty steel helmets being put up to draw your fire; but employ this trick yourself.)

At short ranges, this allows for trajectory and also reduces the tendency to shoot high and miss. If the bullet is too low, a hit may still be scored, for it takes more than a few inches of earth or most other protection to stop it. It should also be remembered that rifle fire will pass through the trunks of small trees, so that a Nazi using one as protection is vulnerable. This point-blank shooting is a desperate game. It calls for the stoutest of hearts and the coolest of heads. But it has several advantages for the Home Guardsman.

If one is in the midst of the enemy, it means that he is usually unable to use his machine-gun, automatic pistols, hand grenades or stick grenades for fear of killing his own men. Similarly, he dare not introduce any field guns which he may have in the vicinity, while of course his dive bombers would be equally useless.

Finally, the average Britisher's brain works quicker than the average German's, which is a telling factor. If things get overwhelmingly terrifying, there is one trick well known to game hunters which can be tried. Take a few deep breaths, and you will find that the muscles and nerves are stimulated and steadied. The ex-rugger player excels in point-blank warfare, for it requires similar qualifications.

LESSONS IN BRIEF

Get among the enemy when he lands: it will be a disagreeable surprise for him.

Bullets travel faster than they can be dodged.

Keep your head by breathing deeply if in a tight corner.

Disperse yourselves, for close formation and men in file are the tommy-gunner's dream.

Shoot fast at disappearing targets.

Aim for the Nazi's navel.

Keep out of sight if you can.

Dive bombers and aeroplane machine-guns are mainly for frightening you; they rarely kill. Ignore them, as far as possible, and keep constant all-round watch for enemy troops creeping up towards you.

CHAPTER FOUR

SHOOTING MOVING SOLDIERS, TRANSPORT AND AIRCRAFT

Practising with Mobile Targets—The Three Secrets of Hitting a Soldier on the Run

I HAVE watched army manœuvres ''somewhere in England,'' and seen men in good defensive positions who did not fire at several attackers who were well within range. On asking the reason, I was told that the defenders did not shoot because the attackers were moving quickly, and they felt it would be unwise to give away their positions, when the chance of killing was so small. This typifies the attitude of many. They feel a rifle is useless except for stationary targets. This is not the case at all, as I hope to prove.

First, however, let me tell you of something which happened in the early days of the Home Guard, when invasion was expected, and many volunteers were jittery and ready to shoot on the slightest suspicion. It was a windy afternoon, and a Home Guardsman was acting sentry, when a young man ran along a road about eighty-five yards away. He challenged but received no response. The Guardsman was not an experienced shot, but he fired at the man's legs, thinking he had little chance of hitting, but knowing that his shot would show he would stand no nonsense. Imagine his surprise when the runner toppled over, wounded in the foot. It later turned out that, on account of the wind, the civilian had not heard the challenge and that he was hurrying to his work. That, however, is beside the point, which is that the sentry hit the runner BECAUSE HE FIRED AT HIM INSTINCTIVELY.

If he had obeyed the text-book and tried to make allowance for the man's speed, the odds are that he would have missed.

Various writers have gone to much trouble to explain just what allowance should be made for a moving target. They will tell you to allow so many inches for a man running across your line of fire, if he is a hundred yards away; so many feet, if he is two hundred yards distant, and so on. Ignore this advice. It is useless, because men run at different speeds, and often they do not run across your line of fire. They may, in fact, be running diagonally, almost straight at you, up a hill, down one, or in some other direction.

Shooting a Nazi on the run is more difficult than sniping at a stationary target, so as a rule, such shots should not be taken at over 200 yards. A really good shot would be able to obtain one hit with every second bullet in most conditions. The secret of hitting a moving target is simple. Follow the target with your aim for a few seconds to judge its speed, then just before firing, quite instinctively and without any conscious allowance, you will find that you swing a little in front of the enemy. Always keep your eye on the target, and for a moving one, on the front of it, so that if you are shooting a running Nazi, focus the front buttons of his tunic.

For shots of less than 50 yards, no forward allowance is required. In firing at moving targets, however, Home Guardsmen should make sure that the rifle follows through. There must be no jerking the rifle forward, or of checking the swing the moment the trigger is released. It is the same principle as following through in golf. For these shots, follow the target for a second or two and then when you have made sure of your aim, pull the trigger.

Instinctively and unconsciously, one realizes that if the bullet is to get home, a forward allowance must be made. Do not, however, try to measure it, because such a thing is impossible. The instinctive mind is quicker than the brain in this matter, and unconsciously the experienced shot will make whatever allowance is required.

Obviously, a man running straight at you is an ordinary and very easy target, as is one running straight away. When running diagonally across your line of fire, even at 200 yards, little forward allowance is necessary. Theoretically, if the target is running right across you at his fastest, at 200 yards, allowance is only a matter of 2 feet. There is neither time, ability, nor necessity to make this adjustment consciously.

Next time the beginner is at the range, he should observe the velocity of a bullet. This can be done by mentally noting when the trigger is released and listening for the noise of the bullet hitting the stop butt. Even at 500 yards, it will be found to be almost instantaneous. This illustrates the terrific speed of a bullet and the infinitesmally short space of time between its discharge and its arrival at the target. In shooting moving targets, one need not worry about the sights. The Nazis will rarely give you any time for that!

To prove that instinctive allowance is easier than conscious effort, it has been found that many men can shoot better in the semi-darkness than in daylight. I myself have often shot running rabbits with a rifle when the light was such that I could only just see the animal's outline. For motor cyclists, military vehicles, etc., the same principles apply. Keep following the target with the rifle, and then swing smoothly ahead of it for the forward allowance, not stopping when the trigger is released. If necessary, reload and repeat the performance.

For aeroplanes at a few hundred yards—it is hopeless to fire if they are over 1,000 yards away— the need for forward swing is greater because of the speed. The actual allowance required is approximately the distance between the first and little fingers of a spread-out hand held at arm's length if the plane is travelling across your line of fire at 300 miles per hour, that is, about 10/12 degrees. The impossibility of judging this consciously will be realized when it is explained that a target moving at this range and speed scarcely allows time to place the rifle to the shoulder without making complicated mathematical calculations.

In war, as distinct from print, there is hardly time

to aim at all, and that is why the whole technique must become so natural that it is carried out without thought.

As with ordinary shooting, there are three secrets of hitting the moving enemy, (1) practice, (2) more practice and (3) still more practice.

The best way to obtain this is to get hold of a .22 rifle, or good air-gun, and go out among the rabbits. Most farmers will gladly allow you to shoot these vermin. If rabbits are not available, hares and rats provide good practice. The advantage of realistic training is that the results can be observed. A quick eye can see where the bullet strikes the ground. This is more simple if the earth is ploughed, as dust is thrown up by the bullet contacting the ground and the shooter can observe if he is aiming too far in front or behind his objective.

Another good moving target can be provided in country districts where there are fast-flowing rivers. A piece of wood or a bottle can be put into the stream and shot at from fifty or a hundred yards, so that results can be observed. In lake districts a moving target can be improvised by making what is known as an otter. This is a boat-shaped piece of wood with a rudder fixed to it, which is set to make it go out into the lake. To this is attached a string which is held by a companion on the bank, who, by running along the shore, causes the otter to travel at the same speed in the water a hundred yards or more out in the lake. The splash of the bullet denotes the result.

For those who cannot obtain such ideal experience, there are other methods of practice. A dog chasing a ball in a garden, for instance, can be aimed at with an empty rifle. Also, aim can be taken at passing cars or cycles from house windows. Another method is to ask a friend to move a long stick, with a handkerchief tied to it, at arm's length in circles over the head. This provides splendid training for the muscles, nerves and eyes. Practice should be carried out not only from the standing position, but also from the kneeling and lying stances. It is not good for the striking pin that the trigger of an empty rifle should be released too frequently, but a few hundred times will not usually do any harm. One cannot, however, overdo aiming practice, but it is not necessary to use the trigger on every occasion.

A few hours of practice is not enough. One must devote considerable time to this training if one is to become proficient. If the time can be spared, work for half an hour a day for a month, and then you will be nearing perfection. In the early days the beginner will find that his arms become easily tired, but he should force himself to carry on, and soon the muscles and nerves will become so strong and steady, and the eyes so accustomed, that training does not exhaust.

The reward for practice is great. It may not only mean saving your life or that of a companion in an emergency, but there is much satisfaction in being able to hit moving targets in whatever form they are . presented. In actual battle, there will undoubtedly be more opportunities for firing at moving enemies

than at stationary ones. Our task is to beat the Nazi
at this game.

LESSONS IN BRIEF

Keep your eye on the target, allow your instincts
and the rifle to do the rest.

Practise aiming at mobile targets thousands of
times.

It is useless firing at long ranges.

Aim for his tunic buttons as he runs across.

Remember to follow through with the rifle.

Shoot straight at targets coming straight at you.

Practise among the rabbits.

Train with home-made otters.

Use other methods of practising.

CHAPTER FIVE

SHOOTING AT NIGHT, IN SMOKESCREENS—
And ARTIFICIAL AIDS TO VISION

Silent Ways of Keeping Contact at Night—
Rehearsal of Plan of Attack

In attacks at night, in moonlight, fogs, mists or smokescreens, the Home Guard, on account of their local knowledge, should be able to inflict punishment on the enemy out of all proportion to anything he can do to them. Such a result will only be possible if the men are trained in this sort of warfare. It is, in fact, probable that night will be the only time at which the Home Guard can attack a superior force. I believe, on account of modern methods, many assaults will be carried out at night which in former days would never have been considered practicable.

In the 1914–1918 war, various ways of shooting at night were developed. In trench warfare, a simple device was employed to repel night assaults. A piece of wire was stretched along the top of the trench under which rifles were placed, so that if the enemy charged he could be fired upon. Similar directional firing may be useful in certain defence positions. For instance, if it was desired to keep a vital point covered, before nightfall two sticks, the shape of catapults, could be so fixed that when

D

the rifle was laid along them, its fire was directed
at the desired spot. Even on a pitch-black night this
would enable either rifles or machine-gun fire to be
used, should it be established that the enemy was
approaching.

Big game hunters have tried painting their sights
with white paint, so that they will show up in
the dark. This, however, is an amateur device,
for, as we have shown, an experienced shot only
requires to see his target in order to be able to
focus, and he can leave the rest to his instinctive
aiming.

Successful night assaults are of value because
they have an especially bad effect on morale. Half
a dozen Nazis killed at night are worth several times
that number killed during the day, particularly if
the attacking forces appear out of the blue, do their
work and vanish, as is possible in darkness.

In shooting in poor visibility, accidents are almost
unavoidable, but the soldier must be trained to
recognize enemies from friends. To this end, he
must be able to identify the enemy from the shape
of his uniform and equipment. With practice, this
becomes possible, the helmet, gas-mask and weapons
of the Nazis differ greatly from ours.

At night, communication between members of
the attacking force is as difficult as it is essential.
There are various different ways of giving and re-
ceiving messages. One is by rubbing two pieces of
sandpaper together to make sounds similar to the
natural noise of the grasshopper. Signals have to
be pre-arranged, and it is well to limit them to a

few well-known commands, such as "advance," "retreat," "keep still" or "open fire."

Another, perhaps better means, is for the leader of the patrol and all the members to hold a piece of string. A pre-determined number of tugs will denote a certain action. In night conditions it is necessary to keep in touch, owing to the risk of getting lost or of mistaking one of your own party for the enemy. Again, a well blacked-out hooded torch, only visible at a few yards, might be employed, provided there was no likelihood of the enemy seeing it. At night, patrols of half a dozen or fewer bold men are generally best, especially if they have worked together before in difficult conditions and proved themselves.

Of course, when a patrol is out, all other sections in your area must be given a rough idea of the expected route, and of the time and place of arrival home.

These patrols at night will be valuable to the Home Guard, because they can accomplish so many things. Their tasks would vary from preventing the enemy from forming up to merely harassing him, or capturing prisoners from whom information could be obtained.

Because it is dark, the patrol should not make the error of bunching and must, of course, use all available cover. They must send forward scouts before the main body advances.

String, wire and even strong thread are excellent means of erecting booby traps to give warning of the approaching enemy. Thread, in particular, is excellent, because the person who trips over it is unaware that he has given an alarm to a sentry perhaps twenty or thirty yards away.

Night is the ideal time for snipers and for those trained in the art of stalking, because sentries can be surprised by this method. Bayonets are, of course, useful for night fighting, but should not be fixed till the last possible moment. Every Home Guard should be trained to fix them silently.

It is obvious that a shot should never be fired at a single Nazi if he can be disposed of by the bayonet, or a blunt instrument, for the demoralizing effect is great when, next morning, a sentry or a patrol is found mutilated. Further, this method, being more or less silent, may not give away the attacker's presence. This variety of warfare calls for great courage, and it is useless sending out the fainthearted. Soldiers are apt to look down on ordinary ·22 rifles and on ·22 air rifles. On account of their comparative silence these are sometimes most useful. With them shoot for the head or heart and you will kill your man.

In moonlight, fogs, etc., the attackers have the advantage. Only those who have been surprised know the terror of it. When an enemy soldier, or a party of them, is caught, they invariably take a few seconds to collect their wits and weapons. It is during this *interim* that havoc can be created. It is the unexpected, the audacious, impossible attempt which almost always succeeds.

Never attack the enemy when he expects to be attacked. For instance, if he has posted sentries, keep away for several hours until they have become bored and tired. Then, having a decoy—a man, or perhaps a dog—to distract his attention, come up behind and finish him off as quickly as possible. If he is guarding a hut or a house, and the inmates hear a noise, they will probably rush out. Coming from the light into the dark, they will be blind for a few seconds, during which your machine-guns, previously placed to cover the exits, can open a devastating fire.

If outnumbered and forced to retreat, always do so singly, so that you cannot be rounded up. A pre-arranged meeting place should have been fixed beforehand, so that you can collect together again.

It must be remembered that sentries are usually covered by another soldier who is hidden. The hidden danger is naturally the greater, and he should be discovered first and then the two can be dispatched simultaneously. The muffled sound of the struggle or the shot, as the case may be, should be the signal for your comrade's attack on the sentry.

When you have to post sentries, both ought, if possible, to be hidden, and it is a mistake to challenge just for the sake of doing so. The command "halt" in itself gives you away, and if you are halting an enemy, he will take care that such a thing does not occur again.

If a single man approaches, let him through and give a signal, by string or other means, to someone in your rear, so that the enemy can be caught from behind, with a bayonet in his ribs. This may appear dirty fighting, but you are dealing with Nazis who know no laws.

Of course, if you can light up your enemy, at the same time keeping under cover or in the dark, better results can be obtained. This raises the question of artificial aids to vision.

The Britisher is good at improvising, and many surprises should be devised and held in readiness for any possible situation. Among the recognized methods of lighting up a target are Very lights, flame-throwers and flares dropped by aircraft over the enemy position. These are useful, but in many situations their employment may be impracticable for one reason or another. There are other methods, for instance the Molotov cocktail with squib attached, thrown into the centre of a Nazi patrol from a concealed position, would give the ambushers an excellent chance of wiping out the enemy. Another idea would be to fix a few safety matches against the striking face of a match-box in some hay or straw beside a road where the enemy were expected to pass. The straw could have previously been soaked with some inflammable substance, so that, at a given moment, a string could be pulled which would cause the matches to ignite, and so set alight the heap of hay, the reflection of which would show up anyone in the vicinity.

These are a few suggestions. There are many others, among which is the use of stationary cars with wire fixed, so that headlamps can be switched on from a concealed position. Admittedly these would be easily extinguished by the enemy, but not before some shots had killed half a dozen of them.

Another point worth mentioning is that if a red light or torch for stopping traffic has to be used at night, it should be held at arm's length, so that if the holder is fired at he has a chance of escaping. Better still is to fix the light to a pole, so that it can be held several feet from the body.

As to the use of passwords at night for returning patrols, these are not always effective because, if the enemy captures prisoners, by third degree he can sometimes make them talk. Then, by using the correct password, he can gain a surprise over the defenders. It is a much better plan to have your sentries concealed and wait till they recognize their own men, either by sight or by a quietly given challenge, to which the answer of a known friendly voice is satisfactory. The old notion of shoot first and ask afterwards, even if you know you have no patrols out, is ridiculous. It gives away your defence position, and may mean the death of a runner from a neighbouring platoon. If bayonets are fixed at night, they should be smeared with mud to prevent their gleaming, also any brass buttons.

It should also be mentioned here that the self-igniting bomb, or burning potato shaws, make quite good improvised smoke generators. These "bombs" can be exploded by rifle fire from a safe distance.

For night fighting, or fighting in smokescreens, the secret of success is to rehearse your plans carefully and only use brave men with initiative. In no other field can the lone hand, if he is experienced, obtain such rewards with so little risk: but he must have everything worked out in advance, including a place where he can retreat and lie low, if need be, for days on end. If you have ever tried to catch a farmyard-raiding fox, you will understand and agree with what I say.

LESSONS IN BRIEF

Pre-arranged catapult rifle rests to cover vital points.

Work out silent methods of keeping in touch on patrol at night.

Never fire if you can use a bayonet.

Keep sentries hidden and don't *shout* "Halt!"

Devise methods of illuminating only the enemy.

Rehearse all plans carefully and advise neighbouring units of your operations.

Scatter separately and meet again at pre-arranged rendezvous if necessary.

CHAPTER SIX

SEEING THINGS YOU NEVER SAW BEFORE

Eye Training and Observation, by Day and Night
How to Organize Your Eyes in Searching Ground

ONE can only shoot what one can see, therefore stimulation of the senses of sight and observation is imperative.

Here is a story to illustrate my point. A famous artist once asked a pupil to examine, during his absence, a fish in a bowl. The student looked at it for a few minutes and then, as the artist did not reappear, he turned his attention to something else. After a few hours, the teacher returned and asked the pupil what he had seen. The reply was that the fish had been thoroughly examined, and that he knew all about it. The artist then proceeded to question him: how many fins had the fish? what was the approximate number of scales and their shape? the size and colour of the eyes, etc.? The student was dumbfounded, for, alas! he had not noticed any of these points.

The painter then rebuked the student and told him to make a fresh examination next day. The following evening he inquired whether the student was ready to be questioned, and was told that a further delay of twenty-four hours would be appreciated, for there was still much which could be profitably studied. Of course, in the first instance, the pupil had merely looked at the fish, and the moral is that even in things which appear commonplace, there is much to be discovered by closer observation. One of the essentials of the good soldier is to become observant, and to see everything around, both by day and by night.

The development of the power of sight and observation are more difficult than many think, and require considerable practice. The soldier must become fish-eyed, and see everything everywhere. One of our most common faults is to look only in one place, and to concentrate the sight on the place where we *think* what we are seeking is to be found. If you are a golfer, you will know what I mean. Most of us have sent a ball into some bush or rough, and searched for it in the place where we are sure it went.

After abandoning the search as hopeless, playing another ball and moving off, we have found the original one many yards from where we thought it landed. That is why in looking for a ball, one should search not only where one thinks it went, but everywhere in the immediate vicinity.

Similarly, in searching ground for the enemy, one must not only concentrate in the likely places, but in the unlikely ones, for it is in the unexpected cover that good soldiers will be found. In moving across ground, the tendency is to look in front, but, of course, that is insufficient. At all times, the soldier should keep a sharp watch, for it is only by so doing that he will see enemies on his flanks or behind him. All this searching can be carried out with the naked eye, but if anything suspicious is seen, glasses can be used for detailed examination.

Your very life depends on the training and quickness of your vision, and the average townsman is at a disadvantage, for his eyes, accustomed to streets and roads, are not experienced in picking out movements and objects in the country. Farmers, poachers, shepherds, etc., are able to see objects in fields, woods and copses which many of us would miss. For instance, a farmer can look over a stubble field and tell that there are partridges in it, while the inexperienced would see nothing at all.

The reason is that the farmer is practised, and the city man is not. When the latter examines the field, he looks from one part of it to another, but the farmer begins at one side, takes a width of twenty yards and searches it in a parallel line to the boundary, right down the edge of the field; then he looks at another strip, and continues his search until he has examined the whole surface. In other words, he organizes his eyes for the job.

In searching ground for the enemy, one should allow the eyes to sweep in a circle right round one. The width of the circle will depend on the nature of the ground. The next sweep should be a wider circumference, and so on, until the whole area to the horizon is systematically searched. Needless to add, the searcher should be invisible for, if there are troops, almost certainly some of them will move, thus betraying their position.

There is no short cut to success except practice

in varying conditions. Fortunately, this training can be done anywhere. As you go about, force yourself to take note of people in the streets. Count the number, for that helps the eyes to register, and develops alertness. With practice, observation becomes an instinctive habit. As you pass a field of hayricks or stooks, count them: count any birds you may see in flight, for you will find that objects which are moving are disconcerting. Train the eye not to be fooled by their antics, but to pick out each bird, or sheep, or whatever you are counting.

This may sound uninteresting, but after a time you will be surprised how much you discover which formerly you did not know existed. You will also note such elementary points as how much more can be seen when looking into the light, or the least cloudy part of the horizon. Practise pacing the distance between you and the object seen. This knowledge is useful for estimating the range and judging how far away troops are from a given point.

In fogs, smokescreens and at night, practice is also required. Here you will discover how much further away things are than they appear to be; and you will also find that more can be seen in inferior light than many imagine. In moonlight it is astounding how far and how much one can observe, especially if the moon is in front of one and high in the horizon.

On even the darkest nights, the soldier should be able to find his way about easily by knowing the lie of the ground. The secret in extreme darkness is, so far as is practicable, to keep looking up. For instance, one can make one's way along the darkest lanes and streets by looking up at the trees or houses on either side.

For such practice, one should have a companion and take turns at acting as enemy. The beginner will be amazed at how much can be observed in the darkest conditions. He will find how easily the face is seen, and how, by lying flat and looking up against the skyline, the human form can be identified even on dark nights. Get your companion to walk into the dark or moonlight, as the case may be, and measure the distance at which he can be observed. Get him to hide in cover, and see if you can find him. Think out various exercises. All this training is elementary, but essential, if you would see before being seen.

The wearing of dark glasses for a few hours before dusk, and the inclusion of as many fats as possible in the diet, are practical aids to seeing at night.

Above all, whether by day or moonlight, learn to take the wide view and do not over-concentrate. Be specially careful to examine windows, walls, trees, and watch out, if in a hedge or wood, you see anything which may resemble a newly made hide.

LESSONS IN BRIEF

Look behind and around as well as in front.

Practice observing at all times to make your eyes alert.

In searching ground, organize the eyes.

Practice at night, and in all atmospheric conditions.

Watch windows, walls, hedges, trees, etc.

Don't over-concentrate—take the wide view.

Observing nature is informative. Birds usually fly off when approached. Crows or wild pigeons in a field generally mean there are no infantrymen around, for these birds are most ''gun-shy.'' Watching the behaviour of farm animals will often provide information of enemy movements.

CHAPTER SEVEN

NOISE: WHAT IT TEACHES AND ITS OFFENSIVE USE

The Art of Analysing Sounds—The Employment of Signals for Silence

To hear without being heard should be a motto of every soldier. He should not only know how much sounds tell the enemy, but what he can learn by listening. By day, and especially by night, in fog or in woods, sounds travel further than many appreciate. In manœuvres on hard ground, by lying with the ear to the earth, and on soft ground, by standing up I have heard enough to tell me nearly all I needed to know about the enemy's whereabouts, intentions and numbers. This would have been impossible if I had made any noise myself, as I should have betrayed my position; for it often happens that by remaining in a concealed position, if necessary for hours, the enemy being confident that there is no one near, gives himself away.

The most common fault in this situation, however, is whispering and breaking twigs. Many imagine that because they whisper instructions no one far off will hear; in reality, a whisper can be picked up by an experienced soldier at perhaps three hundred yards.

Therefore every Home Guard should be trained

to move in silence, and to convey instructions by signs made with the hand or rifle. To signify a move forward, a sweep with the left arm is all that is required. Each man must be trained to signal to the one following him as he moves from point to point. The signs used by motorists are quite sufficient to convey what is needed. The hand waved up and down would mean caution; the raised hand, as by a policeman in traffic, would signify halt, and so on. The rifle held shoulder high, indicating a certain direction, would mean that the enemy had been seen. If there is a large force, it should be moved up and down carefully a few times. These are recognized signals.

While moving through woods, it is necessary to see that the dead branches or twigs are not trodden on and broken, for these sounds carry a long way. The helmet should be covered with cloth, for when crawling through bushes, any twigs coming into contact with the steel will make a metallic sound and betray one's position.

When moving along roads, the softest parts should always be used, and if the invasion comes, it seems to me that the Home Guard should discard their heavy boots. Regular soldiers require these, as they may be walking long distances in all weathers, but the Home Guard will be unlikely to operate far from home. Shoes or boots with rubber soles should be used, or rubber can be fixed to the existing issue. It is doubtful whether the authorities would defray the cost, but since it is a life-saving measure, no one should grudge the outlay. The next time you are out on exercises, just listen to the sounds I have mentioned and observe what a lot can be learned from them. Practice in listening is as important as practice in observing.

The use of cycle patrols is a splendid idea which the Home Guard do not seem to have considered fully. Cycling is faster than walking, more silent than motoring, and ought to be used particularly at night.

The offensive use of sound is a subject which can be profitably studied. One of the best tricks is the employment of farmyard animals. These can be used to mislead an enemy patrol, and divert their attention from you. Or again, by chasing some cattle into a wood, you can draw the enemy into the position you want him to be. Such methods all help to bewilder the opponent, and throw him off his guard. He hears something, investigates, finds only a horse, and naturally thinks he is mistaken. At such times it is a simple matter to prove the correctness of his assumption. Think out plots like these, especially for use on moonlight nights.

Another useful sound generator is a simple mechanism consisting of a piece of wood or tin and a ball of string. This can be placed in a hidden position with a stick support, to which one end of the string is attached. The object is kept in position by the support, and when you wish to create the noise, you only have to pull the string, which allows the tin or board to fall. The Nazi will doubtless try to discover the cause of the sound, and while

E

he is doing so your well-hidden snipers can operate effectively.

Most Home Guard units have some old shotguns and other useless weapons. A good device for decoying the enemy is to place some of these, loaded —for safety's sake the ball or pellets can be removed, leaving only the explosive—in a suitable position. Again a piece of string can be tied to the trigger, and at the opportune moment released. Then when the enemy are disposing themselves for an attack on their supposed opponents, fire can be opened from another position altogether. The enemy will be thoroughly disconcerted, for everyone likes to know the exact position of the opposing forces. These are but a few examples, but it cannot be too strongly emphasized that tricks with sound can be devised in a hundred ways which will scare and muddle the Nazis. Platoon Commanders should take the advice of any practical jokers among their volunteers.

Noise can be most disconcerting and demoralizing; and in this connection, if men are under bombardment, or being dive-bombed, they should stuff their ears with cottonwool. The Chinese use this means of protection; and I have been told that when the Japanese have bombarded a position until there seemed nothing left, and until all ordinary soldiers would have abandoned it, or been raving lunatics, the Chinese have emerged with their rifles, apparently little the worse.

I am often asked what we will do if the Nazis arrive in our uniforms or dressed as civilians.

In my opinion, the best method will undoubtedly be identification by sound—the sound of their voices. When anyone doubtful is seen, he should be immediately covered with the rifle and challenged. Few Germans can speak sufficiently good English to escape detection, and of course, if they are not *bona fide*, it will be possible to shoot before being shot. The challenger should either be concealed, or at least in the prone position. If he has learned how to shoot fast, he will win every time.

LESSONS IN BRIEF

Hear, but don't be heard.

Sound travels further at night, in fog, in woods or valleys.

Don't break twigs or whisper.

Learn to give signals or hand signs.

Walk on the soft part of the road.

Use noise to bewilder the enemy; think out tricks.

Remember that by putting a car or bus into neutral it becomes a silent troop-transport which can be used, especially at night, for "cruising" downhill to attack the enemy.

Sections should practise tactical exercises in complete silence, using only signs or at most whispering.

CHAPTER EIGHT

CONCEALMENT, PERSONAL CAMOUFLAGE, PROTECTION, ETC.

Least Obvious Cover Usually the Best—Good Protective Materials, and Their Use

CONCEALMENT differs from protection in that the former does not prevent one's being killed by rifle fire. In modern war, where the front line may be the vicar's back garden, or the village station fence, concealment is very important. A good soldier should be the personification of the Invisible Man, for if you cannot be seen, you can rarely be shot. The saying, "old soldiers never die," is derived from their ability to make adroit use of cover and protection.

There are some golden rules in the art of seeing without being seen. The first consideration, often neglected in instruction, is that the least obvious cover is usually the best. By that I mean that if a soldier hid behind a hedge, he would probably be found, because that is where he would be expected. But if he reconnoitred the hedgerow first and selected a place right in the roots, where with the possible aid of some personal camouflage, he could conceal himself, the chance of discovery would be remote. No one anticipates finding a man who has wriggled himself into the roots of a hedge.

Similarly, a soldier might be expected to use a hayrick or coil for cover; but if he dug a shallow weapon pit in a field of mown hay and laid a few sticks across, covered with a few handfuls of hay, he would probably escape detection. It would never be thought that so small an amount of cover could conceal anyone.

I have been told that when paratroops first land they shoot up all hayricks, bushes, etc., as a precaution, and irrespective of whether they believe soldiers are hidden in those places. This, however, seems to me an exaggeration, because to do so effectively would require several hundred thousand rounds of ammunition. In any case, the chance of a stray bullet finding you is so remote as to be negligible, provided you lie low, and head on to the enemy.

In action, when a little damage to crops is unimportant, it should be realized that crawling through corn or hay fields enables men to travel for miles, or to conceal fighting or standing patrols with small risk of being discovered, except, of course, if one comes up against the enemy, who will also be trying to use such cover. When that happens, keep still and let him attack you, for when lying in a cornfield one can see an approaching enemy before being seen. The same remarks apply when woods or shrubs are used for cover. There may be times when you have to attack, but try to avoid doing so. In such tight corners, defence is usually the best form of attack.

When surprised, the best thing is to remain

absolutely stationary, even if you are being looked at. It is surprising how often one will escape detection in these circumstances. The slightest movement attracts the eye. Sometimes, when the enemy turns the other way, it may be possible to secure a better position, for instance, to lie flat. Do this very slowly, so as not to attract attention. The need for keeping still, or if some move is necessary, for carrying it out at an imperceptible speed, cannot be over-emphasized. All wild birds and animals instinctively conform to this rule. It is another matter, if one is actually seen, then the urgency of getting into the prone position is obvious.

Trees in foliage have always been used as cover, but sitting up a tree is a risky business, and rarely worth while. There are three reasons for this. Firstly, owing to the trajectory of the shot, the "plunging" fire is less effective; secondly, the enemy will expect to find men up trees; thirdly, if discovered, there is no chance of retreat. There are usually better positions for snipers, though, of course, high trees have their use for observation. As you go about your daily work, think out various hiding places which could be used in an emergency.

There are two ways of crossing short open spaces between cover which provide a reasonable chance of not being seen. One, by the bounding method. In this, a scout dashes across, signals all is clear, and then the remainder of the party dash across, either one at a time, or together, but always several yards apart. This method is useful for crossing roads, etc., especially if haste is necessary.

But the better way is for men to crawl, with at least fifteen yards between them. This takes longer, of course, but has the advantage of probable avoiding detection. The deer stalker knows this well. In it, the secret is keeping flat and *squeezing* into the ground. Progress is slow, because when crawling, the rifle has to be lifted forward quietly and followed every few inches. Of course, when the open ground has been crossed, the men must never collect together, in case of machine-gun fire, bombs or shells.

While crawling, the respirator should be slung, not at the alert, unless information has been received that gas is being used. The reason is that at the alert, the body is raised several inches, which is dangerous. Gas, of course, is not such a deadly weapon. In fact, I understand that some 97 per cent of all cases recover, and with the Service mask the danger is negligible. It can be fixed from the slung position in a second, and the containing bag brought into the alert position later.

A soldier should never allow himself to be seen against the horizon or skyline. He should make use of valleys and shadows whenever possible. All cover is, of course, helpful, but it should never be fired over—as this exposes the shooter—but always through or round. As most men fire from the right shoulder, it will be found easier to shoot round the right side of cover or protection.

In selecting concealment, remember passing planes. If these are seen when in the open, every man should remain stationary in a kneeling or bending position, with the face and hands hidden. In this way, the plane will probably mistake the troops for bushes or stones. If dive-bombed, there is no need for advice, for men will instinctively always fall flat In action, all shining badges and buttons ought to be removed or covered with mud, for their gleam can be seen for miles.

Attention should also be given to personal camouflage. Individual ideas are helpful here. For instance, when stalking an enemy, one can often devise means of hiding one's approach. In crossing a potato field, a handful of potato shaws held in front as one·crawls afford some concealment. Nor should the rifle be neglected; it can be covered with leaves and made to resemble the surrounding country.

A net over the helmet, in which are enclosed a number of leaves or grasses, is a useful idea. Naturally, the face and hands should be darkened. A thick line, made with a piece of burned cork diagonally across the face will break its whiteness, while dark gloves, with the fingers cut off so as not to interfere with shooting, should be worn. These latter also prevent the hands becoming cut or pricked, and keep them warm in cold weather. No one shoots well with frozen hands.

The whole idea of camouflage is to become a part of your surroundings, and everything should be done to this end. I have seen men crossing open spaces merely with their heads and shoulders bent forward. In war, the reward for such laziness is death. Unless open spaces are taken in bounds, the alternative is crawling, keeping the stomach and the chin *always* on the ground.

Protection against machine-gun or rifle fire also requires consideration, and when practicable, concealment should include protection. If you can take up positions behind some solid steel of an inch thick, you are safe. Old girders, railway or tram lines provide a good basis. Naturally, these must be camouflaged against the ground and the air. A house makes excellent protection, but usually the thickness of the bricks is insufficient, for the bullets may pass right through or wear their way through after a time. Therefore, the inside wall should be reinforced with twenty-four inches of sandbags, and on account of their weight it may be necessary to support the floor, especially if it is an upper one. Curtains should be left in the windows so that outsiders are ignorant of what is inside: and if they are to be used as loopholes, the glass should be removed.

It is better, however, to knock loopholes through the walls with a pick, preferably through one which has creeper, as this hides the hole.

Solid stone walls are usually strong enough protection (they can be tested by a rifle bullet), and loopholes can be made in these, but cover them until the moment of action. A piece of cardboard painted over to resemble the rest of the wall can be removed when action commences. It is naturally better if there are a few bushes in front, provided they do not interfere with the line of fire. The idea of defence positions is to catch the enemy at close range, and by surprise. In the event of invasion, most people will allow their houses and garden walls to be used, and the few who would not should be investigated as probable fifth columnists.

Small stones packed between boards a foot apart give splendid protection and can be knocked up quickly at points where the enemy is expected, provided supplies are kept in stock as well as the necessary transport.

Two and a half feet in width of sandbags are safe protection, and oddly enough, fourteen inches of hard coal. When sandbag posts are put up with loopholes, it is imperative that the whole is camouflaged One idea is to build them in bushes, and another to put a stack of straw or hay around them. Alternately, they can be built inside hen-houses or garden sheds—or the latter can be built round them.

On the basis that the best protection is the least likely, a good position could, with the aid of a strong frame, be built under an ordinary heap of coal, since this is highly protective material. I do not imagine even Nazis would expect to find men hidden in coal heaps

The use of dummy, or unused positions, is sound technique, provided they are covered by real defence posts. They will mislead the enemy and possibly draw his fire, as, of course, do false loopholes, which should always be used in occupied positions. Among other well-known tricks is the placing of dummy soldiers, which are specially effective at night. A helmet, something to resemble a rifle, or an old one, and some equipment may suffice to give the illusion Again, a more life-like scarecrow can be put up. Such imitations should be covered by well placed troops so that advantage can be taken if they deceive the enemy.

Lorries, small-wheeled trucks or waggons filled with small stones and pushed into place, after which they are immobilized by the removal of the wheels, make good protective positions for use in emergency.

Every Home Guard should realize that there is a time to fire and a time to hold fire. The tendency of inexperienced soldiers is to blaze away too soon, and as a general rule wild shots at over 400 yards are both a waste of ammunition and an advertisement of position. Whenever possible, wait till the enemy is within 100 yards, especially if you are in a protected position. Then your fire both kills, surprises and demoralizes.

In some instances, it may be wiser to let the enemy pass, for instance, if outnumbered by, say, ten to one, and concentrate on getting information through to another unit, which assuming the telephones are cut, may be possible by a devious route. At other times, it will be best to allow the enemy through and follow him, picking off men from cover as you go. Remember, every Nazi killed is a Nazi fewer. If they come back at you, it is often possible to elude them by some unexpected move, such as ''retreating'' towards him under cover and lying low.

What is the best range at which to fire? If in the open, and armed with rifles against automatic or tommy-guns only, the best plan is to keep the enemy away, for these small arms only have an effective range of up to about 150 yards, owing, in the case of the tommy-gun, to the recoil and shortness of the barrel, and even the automatic, with its extended stock, is not very deadly at long range.

While every Home Guard has to obey orders, there will often be times when, being alone, he must act on his own initiative. That is why he must develop his own plan of action. Long before the invasion, he should have made up his mind with whom he will ''board'' in the event of being cut off, or having to retreat. From his hidden headquarters, which must be with someone whom he can trust, he will be able to sally forth at nights, so long as the enemy is in the vicinity, and do a great deal of damage. A Home Guardsman must never surrender. If cornered, the only thing is to occupy the best cover and protection and fight it out. It is less hard to die if you know you have accounted for several Nazis.

LESSONS IN BRIEF

A good soldier should personify the invisible man.
Hide in hedge roots rather than behind them.
Choose unlikely hiding places.
Dig weapon pits inside cover.
Keep still, for the slightest movement attracts.
Use crops for cover in emergency.
Practice the art of stalking.
Shoot through or round cover, not over.

Hang curtains inside pillboxes so that a dark background will be formed against which there is less likelihood of your head being seen when manning the loopholes.

The reward of laziness in war is death.

When possible, concealment should include protection.

Make dummy loopholes and camouflage sandbags.

Blacken the face in action.

There is a time to fire and time to hold fire.

Don't take long shots for the fun of it.

Never surrender: fight it out if cornered.

CHAPTER NINE

DEADLY AMBUSH TACTICS AND USES FOR SHOTGUNS

Ambushes must be Placed on Both Sides—Some Unpleasant Tricks with Shotguns

AMBUSHES are the result of ingenuity and should be varied endlessly. The surprise element is the factor which counts, and here we shall merely give a few ideas and principles which may stimulate the reader to novel inventions of his own.

In ambushing a road, railway or valley, it is imperative that both sides should be manned, and that the men on either side know the whereabouts of their comrades to avoid shooting each other. Failure to do so means that the moment the ambush opens fire, the enemy will take up a position on the other side, so that a pitched battle ensues. It is a good trick for the defenders on one side to remain concealed, so that the enemy will think he can easily take up position opposite. As he does so, the hidden ambushers can bring their fire to bear. In ambushing a road, another good method is to have four parties in different positions. Two on either side of the road at one point, and two positions on either side at another point about 200 yards ahead. Any enemy scouts should be allowed through, and when the main body comes up, they can be allowed almost to reach the second position. Then the first position can open fire from behind. The first shot fired by whoever is in charge would be the signal for action. In this way, a number of the enemy could be dispatched before he had time to turn about for his attack. When he eventually turned, the forward positions could then open up, again from behind, so that he would be more or less surrounded. Two machine-guns posts should be placed, well back, on either flank, to provide cross-fire, and above all to prevent the enemy getting between the two positions, which would make shooting impossible on account of killing your own men.

The underlying factor in arranging an ambush is to place it where the enemy would least expect it, and to post men in positions ready to counter any moves which he may make when surprised. I always feel it is better to have one really good ambush than a number of small, ineffective ones, which can often be countered by vigorous action. In an ambush there should always be scouts, posted in trees or cover, who could display a small flag or give some signal to denote the approach of danger. At night, carefully dimmed, hooded torches could take the place of flags.

Feigned retreats by a few troops or motor patrols are another means of drawing the enemy into your ambush, also messages written in German on walls purporting to come from fifth columnists.

Ambushes and tricks can be devised in so many ways and places that is useless to try and enumerate them all. Mines which explode on contact, however, are one of the most successful. These can be placed behind front doors or under mats in buildings which the enemy are likely to enter, but, of course, care is required that civilians or our own troops are not caught by them.

Note A.—Similarly hand grenades with strong thread tied to the pin which is *almost* removed can be used so that when the thread is tripped over the lever is released and the grenade explodes. The principle is similar to setting a mousetrap, so care is needed. The grenades should be placed in a concealed position.

Foodstuffs can be left exposed in shops which are covered by soldiers in nearby buildings. Shotguns, loaded with No. 4 or heavier shot, can be placed under an old piece of newspaper, so that they are fixed to fire down a stair or passage likely to be used by the enemy. These can be discharged by a concealed string, either operated by a hidden Home Guardsman, or arranged in such a manner that the enemy will trip over it and thus release the trigger. Local people, or our own military, must be warned of such booby traps.

Ashbin lids placed in roadways will be thought to conceal land mines and may be the means of slowing up an enemy convoy in the vicinity of an ambush.

War is a series of tricks and bluff, and often the most simple methods are the most successful. Sometimes, for instance, a soldier may be obliged to feign death. A bandage and a bottle of red ink come in useful in these circumstances: the bandage can be tied round the head or throat, and the ink spattered over it to represent blood.

Again, it may occasionally be necessary for a Home Guardsman to assume male or female civilian clothing for the purpose of escape. This is legal under international law, provided no arms are carried or used, except for the purposes of personal defence. This is a point of which many are ignorant.

LESSONS IN BRIEF

Surprise is another way to spell ambush.
Man both sides of the road.
Prevent the enemy getting between your positions.
Think out your own ambush tricks.
When necessary, escape in civilian clothes.
War is a series of tricks and bluff.

CHAPTER TEN

TRICKS FOR TANK DESTRUCTION

Prams with Bombs—A New Use for a Steam-roller

WE all know a good deal about tanks, their blindness, etc., and the use of Molotov cocktails and other bombs for their destruction. Indeed, at Tobruk, the former proved most efficacious. There are, however, a few points which I do not feel have been sufficiently impressed.

By far the best time to operate against tanks is at night, for then their field of vision is virtually nil. Again, they have to go into a tank harbour to allow the occupants to eat and rest. When this happens, the Home Guard should be able to cause a great deal of trouble among them and their crews, with the various weapons it has at its disposal.

We all know that if the driver puts out his head, he will soon withdraw it if fired upon. When closed up, a tank has only vision through the gunner's and commander's vizor or slits. These may have bulletproof glass, but even so, by firing at them, this will be splintered so that vision will become impossible, and the tank temporarily disabled.

The ideal weapon for this purpose is the shotgun, and if by chance the slits are open, pellets will enter the tank and prove most unpleasant for the occupants.

The placing of dummy or live mines, which will make the driver dismount to investigate, is an excellent method, for then he can be fired upon. Similarly, good road blocks will hold up a tank. The method of rolling a tree across the road seems to me inadequate, as a tank shell would soon smash the trunk to smithereens, even if the vehicle itself was unable to push its way through. Several trees, one behind the other, would be a better obstacle, for the tank would be forced to slow up and would not have enough momentum to carry it through.

Another useful trick would be to place an old-fashioned steam-roller on a hill up which the enemy tank or armoured vehicle was likely to pass. When it was fifty yards away the steam-roller, or even a heavy motor-lorry well laden with stones, could be released to charge. This could be arranged by fixing a wire to the brake handle and operating from a hidden trench. A narrow road or street would require to be selected, so that the enemy could not evade this obstacle.

If nothing else were available, an ordinary farm-yard cart, loaded with hay, and so fixed that it could be released by pulling a wedge from under the wheel, could be made to charge the oncoming vehicle. The impact would cause the hay to spread over the tank and blind it, while the Molotov cocktail throwers could operate simultaneously. In fact, if the hay were soaked with inflammable liquid, fantastic as it may seem, it should be possible for the attackers to run up and put a match to it.

An idea for getting a mine or bomb nicely near a tank is to fit it into a child's pram, and pass this baby down the hill to its new foster-parent. Dozens of such tricks, all very demoralizing for the enemy, can be devised by a little hard thinking.

At school I remember being warned that if charged by a bull, I must throw a coat over its horns and blind it. In the same way, a tank could be blinded, in preparation for a Molotov attack, by the simple device of sewing a few bedsheets together, fixing a wire through the top, and placing this contraption across the street. At the moment of the tank's approach, the two ends of the wire could be pulled from some hidden and protected elevated position, such as an upper window, so that a hood would descend on the tank. It is, of course, necessary to release the wire at the moment of impact.

It would be useless to hang the sheets out previously, as the tank would merely shoot at the wire or rope, where it was fixed to the walls. When thoroughly blinded, its destruction should present no difficulty.

LESSONS IN BRIEF

Go after tanks in the dark.
Don't despise the Molotov cocktail.
Keep a few shotguns on hand.

Sow dummy mines, as well as live ones.

Make steam-rollers and heavy lorries charge tanks on hills.

Use prams or children's toys for carrying bombs or mines to enemy vehicles.

Above all, use the imagination, and think out your own tricks.

CHAPTER ELEVEN

SOME COMMENTS AND THE NEW DISCIPLINE

Outspoken Advice to Men and Officers—Dead Methods Versus Living Ones

THE remarks in this chapter are based upon what I have seen and upon conversations with members of the Home Guard all over the country.

The formation of the Home Guard was a masterstroke, and despite what certain people think, there is so much that is splendid about the organization that it is with hesitation that I make any criticism. When I do, it is without malice and in the hope that at least some of the remarks may be helpful.

In the past, there has been much grumbling about lack of modern equipment. This, however, was due to three reasons, apart from the obvious one of providing the regular Army with the tools of war. The Greeks and Abyssinians had to be supplied with materials; the fighting forces of our various Allies had also to be equipped, while the Atlantic sinkings have undoubtedly consigned to the bottom of the sea much of the material intended for the Home Guard.

With the Greek and Abyssinian campaigns over, and the Free Forces now equipped, the future augurs better. Once the U.S.A. comes into the naval war, which appears to be likely, the last difficulty will be largely obviated. We can therefore look forward to better instruments of war.

I make a special appeal to our chiefs to secure for us larger quantities of anti-tank bombs, land mines and hand-grenades; and especially smoke bombs and generators, which would be most useful to the Home Guard since they are without heavy guns or other long-range weapons. Smoke screens would enable us to protect ourselves for the short-range attacks which we shall have to make in the event of invasion, and for which the country is so well suited.

Again, many members possess Mausers and other German weapons which are trophies of the last war, but have little or no ammunition for them. I understand there is plenty in the country, which was taken from Germans resident here before the war, while surely some could be brought from the booty captured in Africa. It is quite time this was made available.

Another matter calling for urgent attention is that of making better arrangements for stored petrol reserves and transport for volunteers in case of emergency. While undoubtedly it will be possible to requisition many cars and vehicles, arrangements in advance with the owners would save considerable trouble. But these would be little use without sufficient petrol, and the arrangements which have been made in this connection seem to me inadequate. The larger Home Guard units should also have a few armoured fighting vehicles.

Quick transport will be most vital for the Home Guard. Men cannot fight their best if they have had to walk or run to the scene of battle, but if arrangements have been made with good drivers to rush reinforcements wherever required, the transport problem will have been solved.

As everyone knows, one of the disadvantages of the Home Guard is that it contains so many men of different ages, and even more serious, of different degrees of fitness. This matter should be tackled and solved. Possibly in all units, certain groups could be formed. The less fit could be detailed for the more defensive roles, while the more fit should be given the tasks of attack and those which call for physical strength, such as fighting patrols, night assaults, etc. In other words, each platoon should have a force of shock troops, carefully selected for their qualities.

Difficulties in connection with discipline are perhaps the foremost question in the Home Guard today. The faults are certainly not all on one side. From time to time, fatuous statements have appeared in the Press and elsewhere which have conveyed the impression that the Home Guard is a sort of come-as-you-please affair. At first there were to be no officers, and all the men were to be equal. This, of course, soon proved impossible. As everyone knows, someone must have authority if muddle and confusion are to be averted.

Again, because it is a volunteer force, some of the soldiers appeared to imagine they could disobey orders; but if a man volunteers for the Army, he has not the right to do as he pleases. It is the same in the Home Guard. Orders must be obeyed, and if any complaints of unfairness have to be made, they should be conveyed to the proper quarter later.

The clause allowing men to resign at fourteen days' notice is generous, but advantage should not be taken of it. After all, we joined the force to win the war. Men should not therefore resign for petty or personal reasons. In fact, it should be pointed out to those who resign that by so doing they forfeit their weapons, which would be most useful in the event of invasion. When it is realized that the Nazis would probably shoot all men whether in uniform or not, men will be less inclined to resign. A number of Home Guards seem to think they are in the force as a favour to their country, when in truth they are in it for their own and their country's protection.

Commanders must make examples of insubordination, for it cannot be tolerated in any fighting unit. Those who refuse to turn up at parades without good cause should be warned, and then dismissed from the force; for such individuals are only a source of trouble now, and if there were an invasion later, would be a source of danger to their fellows. Discretion, of course, must be shown here, bearing in mind that it is easier to dismiss a man than to get him back again.

Basing my comments on what I have heard from all over the country, it can safely be said that where there have been resignations, they are usually symptoms of something else. The faults are by no

means all on one side. In certain instances the men
have been bored and angered by some of the
regulations and training.

The Home Guards are, in the main, highly intel-
ligent and patriotic men; and, here and there, there
has been a tendency to treat them as children and
expect them to play at war. As one friend in a west
country platoon put it, "We are treated far too
much as sheep by goats."

The rank and file do not like stupidity. Sometimes,
instructions have been given one day and contra-
dicted the next. We read in the Press that on no
account is a soldier to clean his buttons as their
gleam will be visible to hostile aircraft, and the
following week we are told that all brass must be
kept shining. Again, instructions are given about
pickets or patrols one day, and for no apparent
reason altered twenty-four hours later when all
arrangements have been made.

As I remarked to a Scottish commander, it would
seem as if those at the top had too little to do, so
decided to make some alterations, just for the fun
of the thing. I may be wrong in this, but if so, why
are we not informed of the reason for the apparently stupid changes in the orders received?

Then there has been an excess of drill, and too
many changes in drill orders. One day we are told
to fall in in one manner, and the next, in another.
The Home Guard has no time for that sort of nonsense. Arms drill, dress competitions and even
shooting competitions, which after all only give experience to those who are already good shots, are

devised with the object of creating discipline. Many
Home Guards are sick to death of hearing such
commands as ''Slope arms,'' ''Quick march,'' etc.
That was the manner of teaching discipline in the
Boer War. It will not kill Nazis, and the men know
it. That is not the way to get the best out of men.
History confirms that highly drilled armies lose
their wars, because drill deadens originality and
reduces courage.

The modern method of providing discipline is to
develop initiative and the fighting spirit, and the men
are anxious for it. Every Home Guardsman realizes
what he is up against, and wants a more realistic
training, such as certain commanders provide.

Discipline can be instilled with half, even quarter,
of the drill and ten times the practical training. All
over the country men have told me that they want
more difficult tasks such as night training, etc.
Discipline and self-confidence will be established if
these methods are employed.

The right way to create discipline is to set men to
carry out the almost impossible. Give them hard
jobs to accomplish, and the thrill of achievement
will spur them on: give them mountains to assault
and rivers to ford in record time. Let them practise
unarmed fighting, felling trees, and *whatever they
are likely to have to perform in action*. When they .
are tired out, call for still greater efforts, and the
men will be found willing. The use of strength
increases strength. ''Unto him who hath, more
shall be given.'' All realistic exercises bring out
discipline and make the men feel their time is not

being dissipated. Those who are not so fit may have to be excused, or given less strenuous jobs. Perhaps some physical training may improve their condition. This is the new method of engendering discipline. Men will follow their leaders better if they admire them rather than fear them. It is the method of love versus hate. In this way the men will realize of what the human frame is capable, and become thoroughly prepared and conditioned for whatever may lie ahead.

One might describe the modern technique of developing discipline as the Churchillian against the Victorian. The living against the dead. The old-fashioned shouted commands versus the spirit and will of men.

In the main, I personally have the greatest confidence in the Home Guard. In a few isolated districts there is room for improvement such as I have described; but if invasion comes, the public can be assured the Home Guard will rise to the occasion.

Our task will be to attack the Nazis by day or by night. In moonlight, or in starlight; at dusk or at dawn. We must fight in companies, or if they are broken up, in bands. We must fight together or, if necessary, alone. If we retreat, it must be for another attack. If we have to lie low for a time, then we must rise again. But we must never give in until the last Nazi on our soil is dead.

LESSONS IN BRIEF

Don't resign for petty reasons.
All orders must be obeyed.
Things are improving now.
Those with stripes remember that those without
    may be better men.
Achieving the impossible develops discipline.
Always attack and never surrender.